First paperback edition June 2022

ISBN (paperback): 978-1-954041-16-5
ISBN (hardback): 978-1-954041-17-2

Published by Creative Sound Press
www.creativesoundpress.com
publishing@creativesoundpress.com

creativesoundpress.com

Grouping Sound

Charlene A. Ryan

For Matthew, Aiden, Audrey Anna, and Amelia Claire.
May groups of glorious sounds permeate your lives.

How to use this book

Each 2-page spread comprises unique works of art designed to represent the grouping of musical sounds – otherwise known as meter. At first, the groupings represent simple unchanging meters – groups of three or four or six, as are often found in musical selections. Later, there are groups of five and seven, less common in some musical circles, but important for building musical flexibility and interest, and for solidifying the concept of musical groupings. Finally, there are groups that represent changing meters, a not uncommon component in musical literature that is often overlooked in discussions and practice of the concept. The artwork provides an aesthetic impetus for engaging children in vocal and instrumental exploration and, importantly, provide clear visual cues as to the emphasis assigned to strong and weak beats. Encourage children to clap, tap, walk, talk or otherwise create the sounds that they hear in the images and to think about how the sounds within one set of images differ from the others. Ask them to create rhythms and melodies that work within each set of images. Then, invite the children to combine their musical and artistic skills by creating artwork to represent meter in the music they create.

PAT pat PAT pat
PAT pat PAT pat...

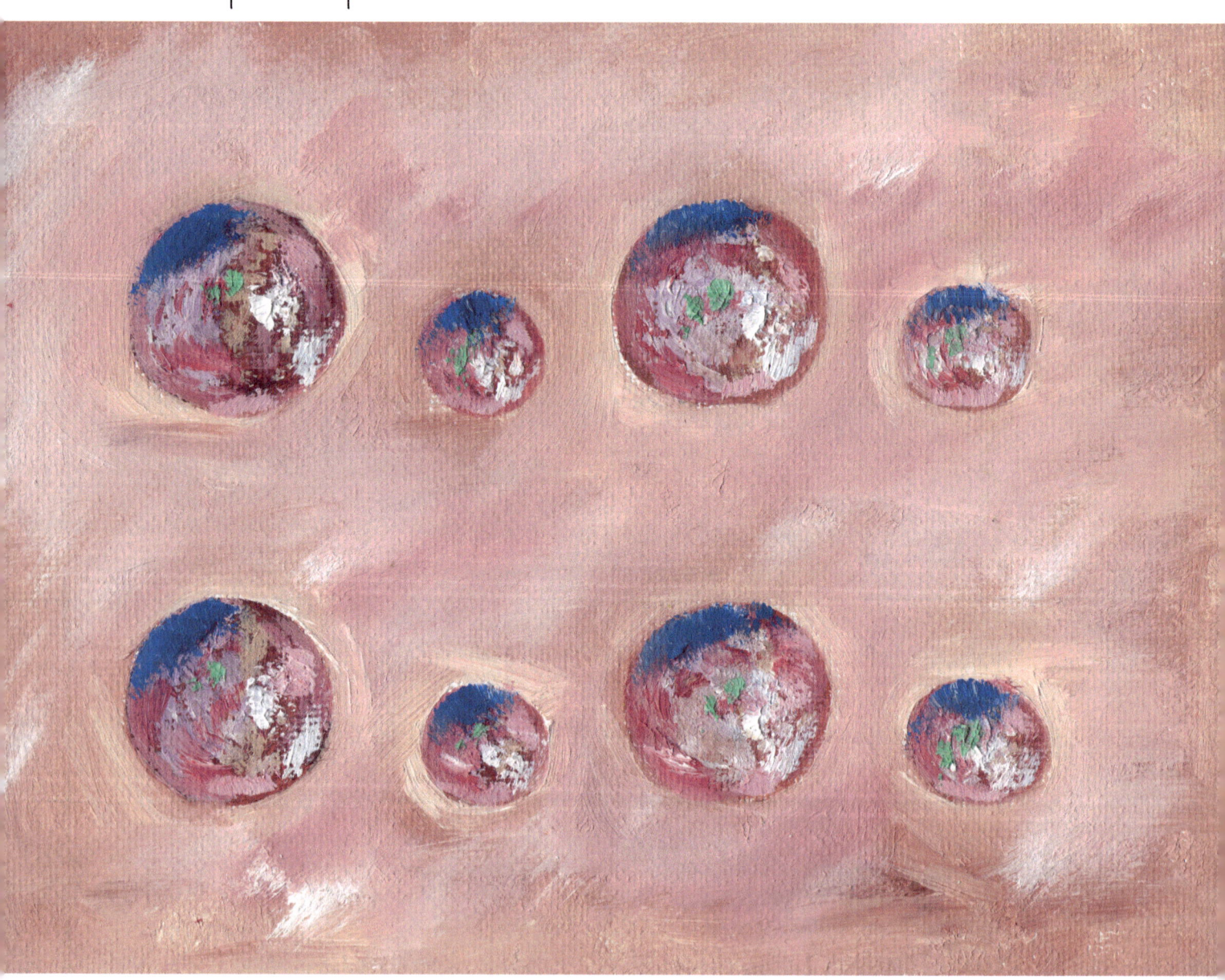

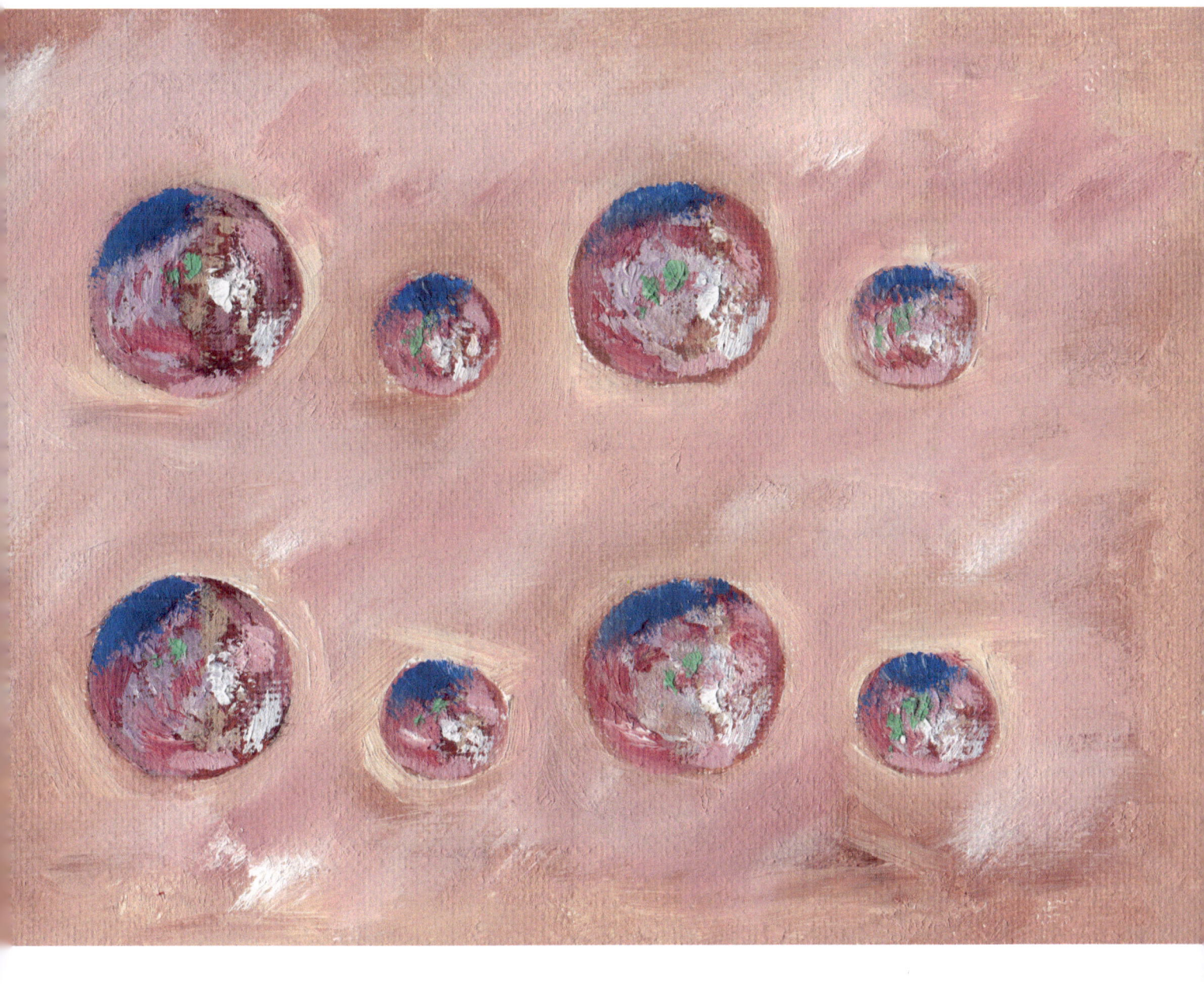

CLAP clap clap
CLAP clap clap...

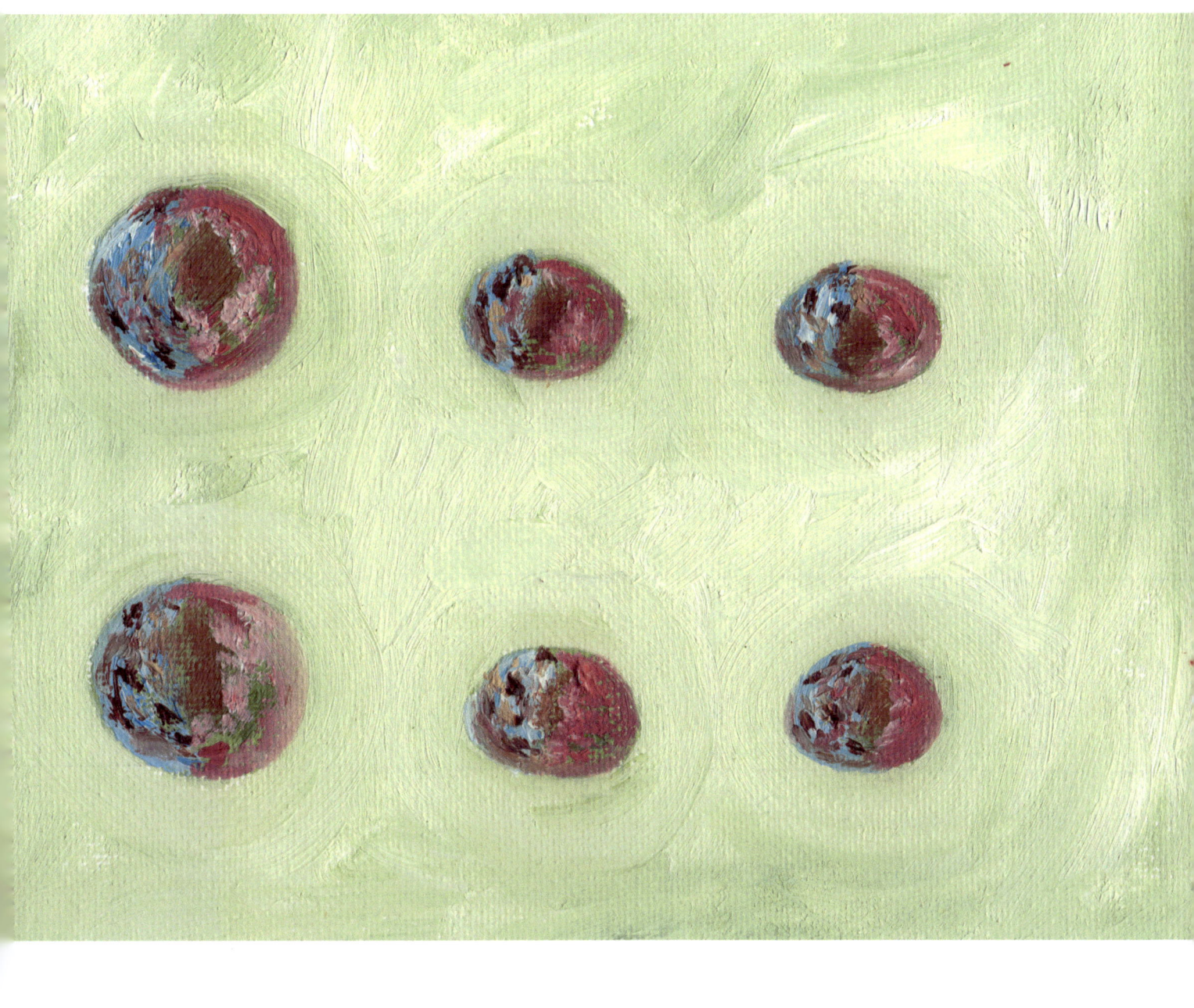

TAP tap tap tap
TAP tap tap tap...

STEP step step step step
STEP step step step step...

PAT pat pat PAT pat pat
PAT pat pat PAT pat pat...

CLAP clap clap clap clap clap clap
CLAP clap clap clap clap clap clap...

TAP tap
TAP tap tap...

STEP step step
STEP step step step...

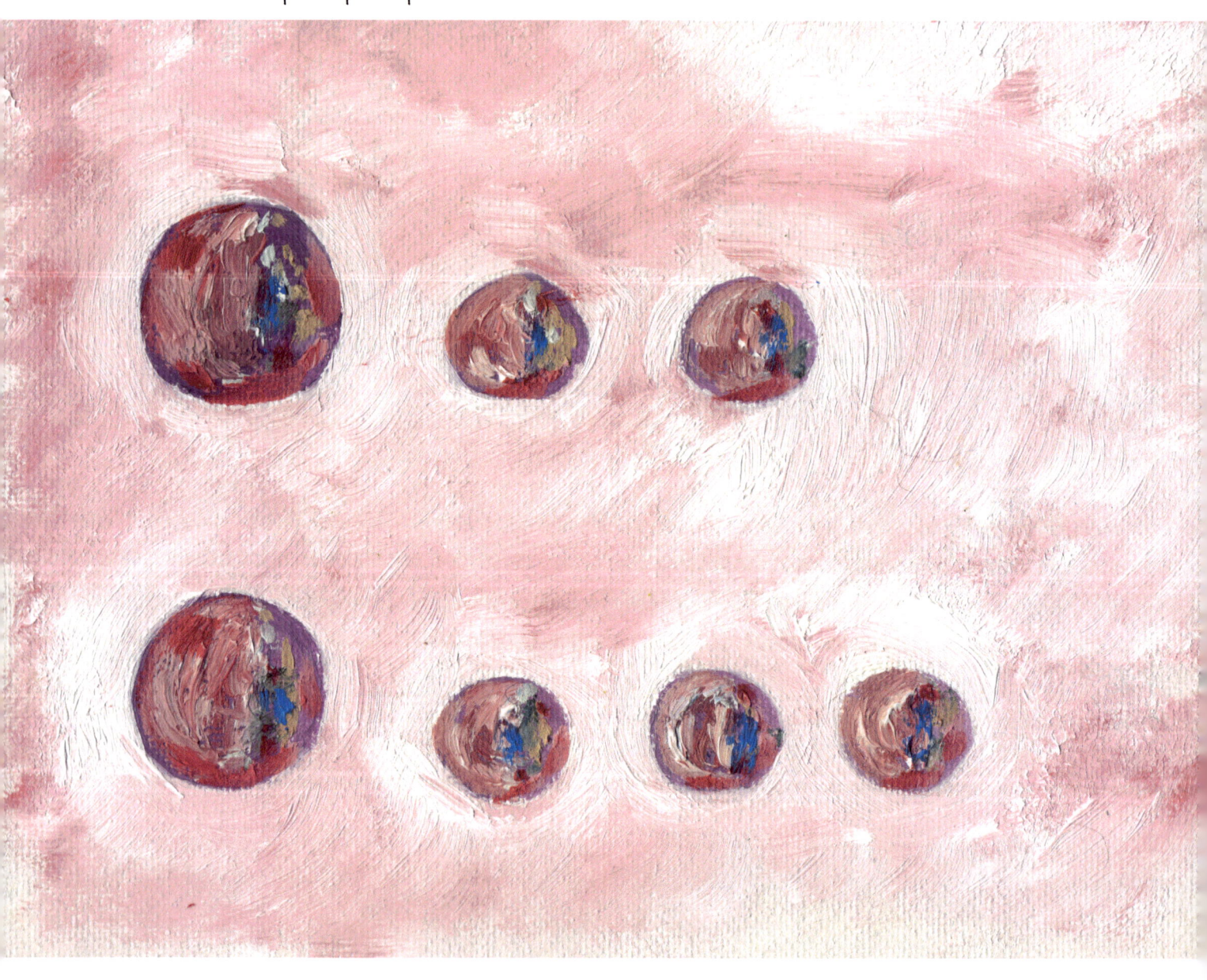

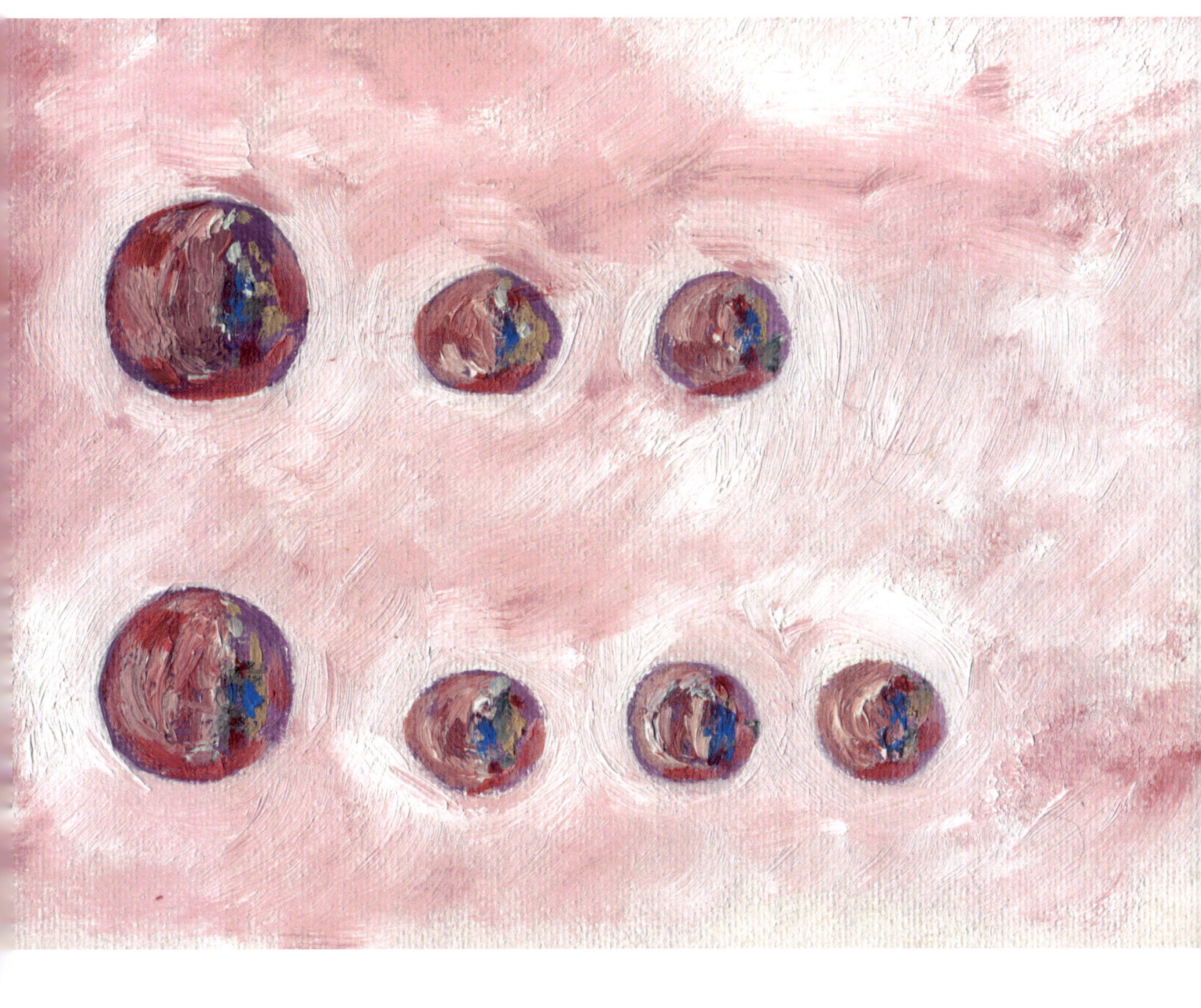

PAT pat pat pat
PAT pat pat pat pat...

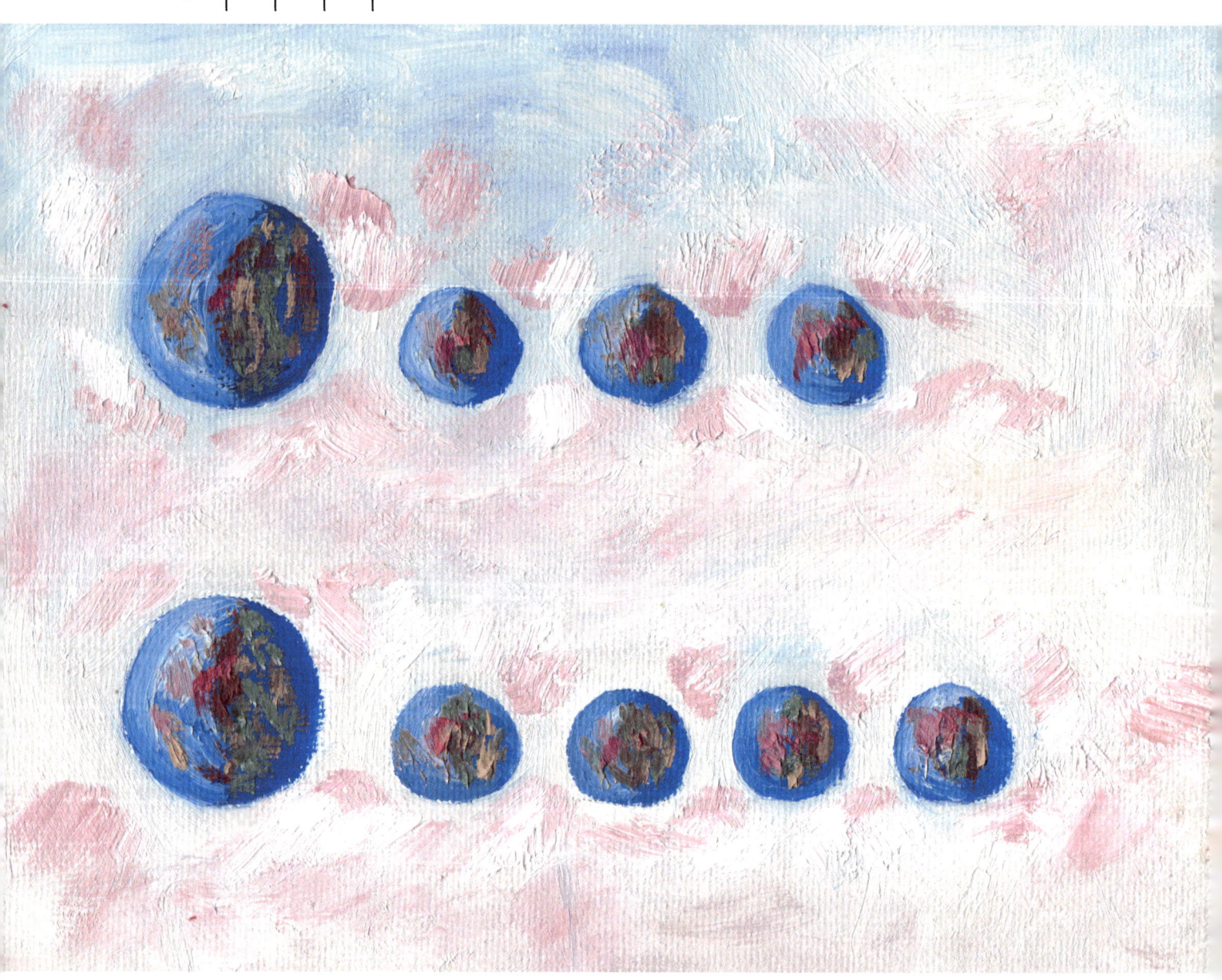

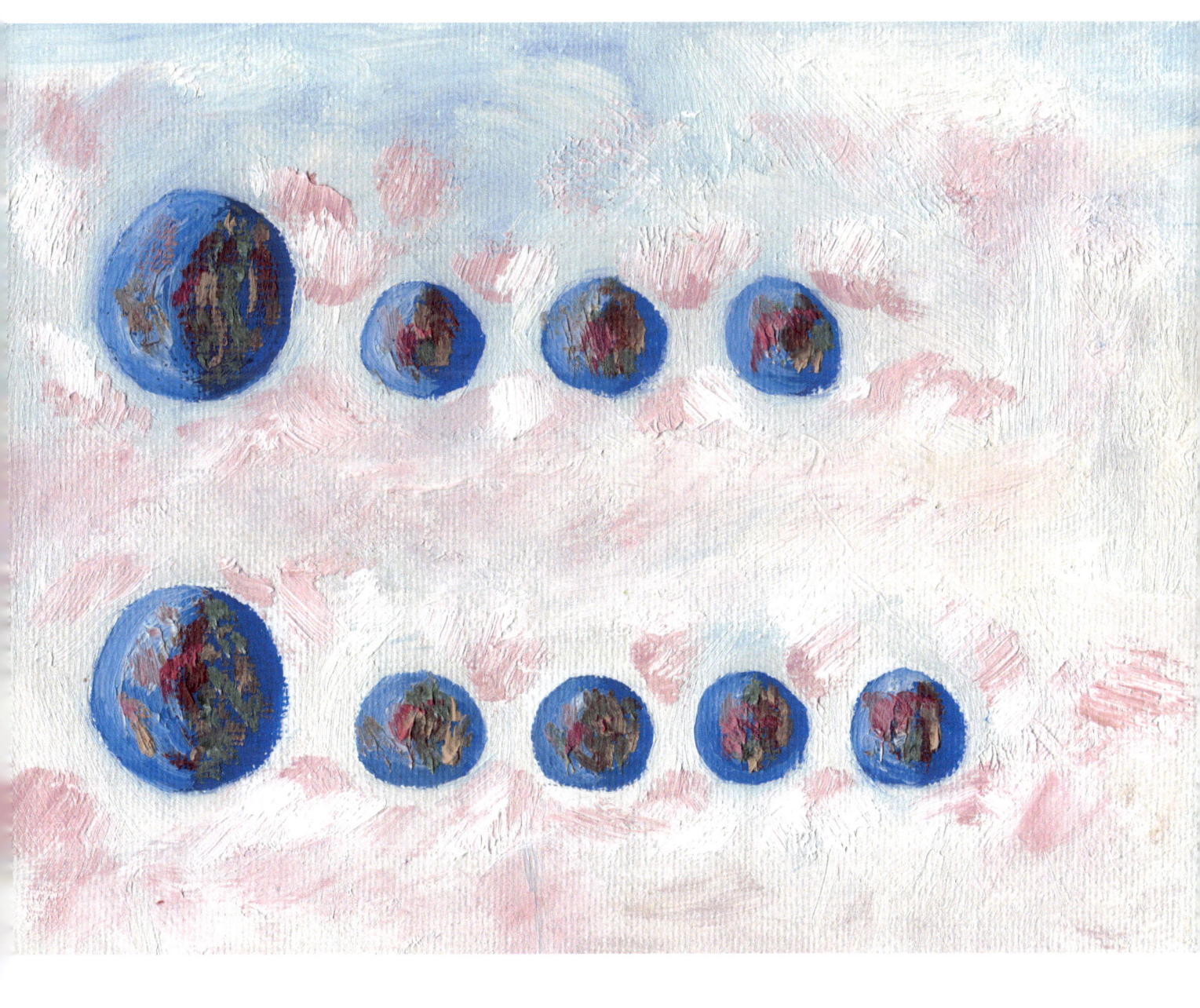

CLAP clap CLAP clap
CLAP clap clap clap clap...

TAP tap TAP tap
TAP tap tap tap...

STEP step step
STEP step step step step...

Charlene A. Ryan is a musician, painter, writer, and mom. She has spent most of her life behind an instrument and in front of an audience of one kind or another.

Other books by Charlene include:
Up and Down Sounds
Layers of Sound
Sections of Sound
Big and Small Sounds
Hannabelle's Butterflies
The Milk Crate Club
Katherine Lost

To learn more about Charlene and her work, visit www.charlenearyan.com

www.ingramcontent.com/pod-product-compliance
Lightning Source LLC
Chambersburg PA
CBHW041606120626
46551CB00002B/327